Contents

Transport and
Communications

London: H M S C

Researched and written by Reference Services, Central Office of Information.

© Crown copyright 1992
Applications for reproduction should be made to HMSO.
First published 1992

ISBN 0 11 701698 5

HMSO publications are available from:

HMSO Publications Centre
(Mail, fax and telephone orders only)
PO Box 276, London SW8 5DT
Telephone orders 071-873 9090
General enquiries 071-873 0011
(queuing system in operation for both numbers)
Fax orders 071-873 8200

HMSO Bookshops
49 High Holborn, London WC1V 6HB
(counter service only)
071-873 0011 Fax 071-873 8200
258 Broad Street, Birmingham B1 2HE
021-643 3740 Fax 021-643 6510
Southey House, 33 Wine Street, Bristol BS1 2BQ
0272 264306 Fax (0272) 294515
9-21 Princess Street, Manchester M60 8AS
061-834 7201 Fax 061-833 0634
16 Arthur Street, Belfast BT1 4GD
0232 238451 Fax (0232) 235401
71 Lothian Road, Edinburgh EH3 9AZ
031-228 4181 Fax 031-229 2734

HMSO's Accredited Agents
(see Yellow Pages)

and through good booksellers

Photo Credits

Numbers refer to the page of the illustration section (1 to 8):
London Transport p. 1 (bottom); British Rail p. 4 (top); Adrian Meredith p. 6 (top);
Post Office p. 8 (top); BT p. 8 (bottom).

[Front Cover] British Rail (top); Post Office (left) .

Introduction

Major improvements in transport and communications in Britain[1] have resulted from the construction of a network of motorways, the extension of fast inter-city rail services, expansion schemes at many airports and investment in modern communications equipment. Transport policy rests on the fundamental aims of:

—promoting economic growth and higher national prosperity;

—ensuring a reasonable level of personal mobility;

—improving safety;

—conserving and enhancing the environment; and

—using energy economically.

 The Government has an important role in assisting road transport, in that the building and maintenance of trunk roads is its direct responsibility. In most other areas of transport and communications, the Government's responsibility is largely that of regulating others; there are many government agencies and bodies concerned with the regulation of transport and communications. The role of the state has been reduced in recent years, with the privatisation of large parts of the transport and communications system which were formerly in state ownership. Major privatisations in recent years include:

---

[1] 'Britain' is used informally in this booklet to mean the United Kingdom of Great Britain and Northern Ireland. 'Great Britain' comprises England, Scotland and Wales.

—the British Airports Authority;

—British Airways;

—British Telecommunications;

—the British Transport Docks Board;

—the National Bus Company;

—the National Freight Consortium; and

—the Scottish Bus Group.

Monopolies have also been discouraged: for example, competition has been introduced in telecommunications, with Mercury Communications providing fixed telephony services, and other companies providing mobile telecommunications. The Government intends to privatise British Rail and London Buses. The opening up of British Rail routes to other service providers is also being studied. The Government intends to introduce greater competition into telecommunications (see pp. 64–5) and postal services (see pp. 78–9).

Britain is taking an active part in the European Community's development of a common transport policy. Liberalisation of international transport within the Community will continue to develop after the completion of the single market in 1992. There will also be pressure for greater harmonisation in areas such as vehicle safety standards.

Central government spending on transport is considerable: budgeted expenditure on transport for 1992–93 is £6,955 million, including support for local authorities and the external financing limits (government grant and borrowing limits) of public corporations such as British Rail. Users' expenditure on transport, including taxation, in Britain totalled an estimated £112,016 million in 1990. The transport sector is a major employer—in December

1991 there were 915,000 employees in transport in Great Britain, with another 447,000 employees in the manufacture of motor vehicles, parts and other transport equipment. There were 404,000 employees in postal services and telecommunications. These figures do not include the self-employed, such as small hauliers.

This booklet describes the major sectors of Britain's transport and communications industry and covers government policies towards them.

General Trends

Travel in Great Britain rose by 36 per cent between 1980 and 1990 (see Table 1). Travel by car and taxi rose by 42 per cent and air travel expanded rapidly. Rail travel also increased. However, recently, travel by motor cycle and by bus and coach has been declining, and travel by pedal cycle has changed little. Car and taxi travel accounts for 85 per cent of passenger mileage within Great Britain, buses and coaches for about 6 per cent, rail for 6 per cent and air less than 1 per cent. International travel has also been increasing (see Table 2).

Table 1: Passenger Transport in Great Britain 1980–90

Thousand million passenger kilometres

	1980	1985	1990
Buses and coaches	45	42	41
Cars and taxis	395	439	561
Motor cycles	8	8	7
Pedal cycles	5	6	5
Rail	35	36	41
Air	3	4	5
Total	491	535	660

Source: Department of Transport.

Table 2: International Passenger Travel to and from Britain 1980–90

Thousand visits

	1980	1985	1990
Visits to Britain:			
by air	7,323	9,413	12,807
by sea	5,098	5,036	5,208
British residents' visits abroad:			
by air	10,748	13,732	21,468
by sea	6,759	7,878	9,710

Source: International Passenger Survey.

Car ownership has also risen substantially, and 67 per cent of households in Great Britain have the regular use of one or more cars, with 23 per cent having the use of two or more cars in 1990. At the end of 1990 there were 24·7 million vehicles licensed for use on the roads of Great Britain, of which 20·2 million were cars (including over 2·6 million cars registered in the name of a company); 2·2 million light goods vehicles; 482,000 other goods vehicles; 833,000 motor cycles, scooters and mopeds; and 115,000 public transport vehicles (including taxis).

Roads

Total traffic for 1990 was 407,000 million vehicle-km. The total road network in Great Britain in 1990 was 358,000 km (222,000 miles). Trunk motorway accounted for 2,993 km (1,860 miles) of this length, less than 1 per cent, and trunk roads for 12,700 km (7,900 miles, or about 3·5 per cent). However, motorways carry

Table 3: Road Length

Kilometres

As at 1 April 1990	Public roads	All-purpose trunk roads and trunk motorways	Trunk motorways[a]
England	273,136	10,823	2,638
Scotland	51,601	3,145	234
Wales	33,297	1,699	120
Northern Ireland	24,081	2,306[b]	112
Britain	382,115	17,973	3,104

Sources: Department of Transport, Northern Ireland Department of the Environment, Scottish Office and Welsh Office.

[a] In addition, there were 68 km (42 miles) of local authority motorway in England and 24 km (15 miles) in Scotland. In April 1990, 108 km (67 miles) of trunk motorway were under construction in England, and 11 km (7 miles) in Scotland.

[b] Motorway and class A roads.

over 15 per cent of all traffic and trunk roads about 17 per cent. Combined, they carry over half of all heavy goods vehicle traffic in Great Britain (see map, between pp. 44 and 45).

Administration

Responsibility for trunk roads, including most motorways, in Great Britain rests in England with the Secretary of State for Transport, in Scotland with the Secretary of State for Scotland and in Wales with the Secretary of State for Wales. The costs of construction and maintenance are paid for by central government. The highway authorities for non-trunk roads are:

—in England, the county councils, the metropolitan district councils and the London borough councils;

—in Wales, the county councils; and

—in Scotland, the regional or islands councils.

In Northern Ireland the Northern Ireland Department of the Environment is responsible for the construction, improvement and maintenance of all public roads.

Public Sector Road Programme

The Government has a major programme to improve motorways and other trunk roads. In late 1991, some 70 trunk road and motorway schemes were under construction in England, costing £1,400 million, while over 400 schemes were in preparation. Important schemes in progress or proposed include the M1–A1 link, the upgrading of the A1 to motorway standard as far as Newcastle-upon-Tyne and widening of several existing motorways. Bypasses and relief roads account for over one-third of the programme, which also includes projects intended to increase the traffic capacity of major through routes and to improve junctions on heavily used roads. In 1992–93 the Department of Transport is supporting 311 major local authority road schemes, the majority of which are bypasses or relief roads.

Road communications in Wales are expected to benefit from the second Severn crossing (see p. 9) and improvements to the M4 motorway. Other priorities in Wales are improvements to the coast road in north Wales. These include the construction under the Conwy estuary of the first immersed tube road tunnel to be built in Britain, opened by the Queen in October 1991. Other roads important for industrial redevelopment are also being upgraded.

The key priorities within the programme in Scotland include the upgrading of the A74 to three-lane motorway standard and completion of the central Scotland motorway network. These routes provide links for commerce and industry to the south and Europe. The programme also includes completion of the dual-carriageway improvement between Stirling and Aberdeen. Other planned improvements include a series of 'route action plans' designed substantially to improve safety and journey times on specific major routes.

In Northern Ireland the emphasis is on improving arterial routes, constructing more bypasses, and improving roads in the Belfast area, including the construction of a new cross-harbour link planned for the mid-1990s.

Privately Financed Roads

The Government is encouraging greater private sector involvement in the design, construction, operation and funding of roads. A framework for encouraging privately funded schemes is provided in the New Roads and Street Works Act 1991. These procedures broadly mirror those for the authorisation of public roads and include public consultation and a possible public inquiry. Private sector operators would be required to produce an environmental impact assessment, which could also be considered at any public inquiry.

An example of such a scheme is the Birmingham Northern Relief Road, the first overland toll route in Britain in modern times. The selection of Midland Expressway Ltd (MEL) as the builder and operator was announced in August 1991. MEL is a joint venture of Trafalgar House and Italstat, and has signed a memorandum of agreement with the Government to design, finance, build and operate the route. The proposal is for a 48-km (30-mile) dual three-lane motorway round the north-east of the West Midlands conurbation to relieve the M6 motorway. Tolls would probably be about £1.50 for cars and £3 for lorries, at 1990 prices. The route would cost about £260 million to build.

Other privately funded schemes recently completed or soon to be undertaken include:

—a crossing of the River Thames at Dartford, linking into the M25 London orbital motorway, opened to traffic in autumn 1991;

—a second crossing of the River Severn, which is expected to be completed by early 1996; and

—a bridge between the mainland of Scotland and Skye, for which a tenderer has been chosen.

The Government proposes to hold a competition for an orbital route to complete the motorway box around the West Midlands conurbation. A new crossing of the Tamar estuary at Plymouth and a link between the M25 and Chelmsford (Essex) have also been recognised as suitable for private finance.

Licensing and Standards

Official records of drivers and vehicles are maintained by the Driver and Vehicle Licensing Agency, based in Swansea in south Wales. It holds records on 34 million drivers and nearly 25 million licensed vehicles in Great Britain. In April 1990 the Agency began to issue a new harmonised European Community driving licence.

Table 4: Motor Vehicles Currently Licensed, Great Britain

Thousands

	1980	1985	1990
Private and light goods	16,301	18,161	21,989
Motor cycles, scooters and mopeds	1,372	1,148	833
Public transport vehicles	110	120	115
Goods	507	582	501
Other vehicles	909	1,146	1,255

Source: Department of Transport.

New drivers of motor vehicles are required to pass a driving test before being granted a full licence to drive. The Driving Standards Agency (DSA) is the national driver testing authority, and runs a network of 510 test centres where the driving test, which lasts about 35 minutes for cars and motor cycles and 70 minutes for buses and lorries, is administered. About 2 million driving tests are applied for each year. The test includes some 25–30 minutes of driving on the road, during which the learner must demonstrate competence to drive in normal traffic conditions and must perform certain specified exercises, such as reversing round a corner, reverse parking or turning in the road. The bus and lorry test includes some off-road manoeuvres. Candidates are asked questions about motoring matters, including the Highway Code, a booklet which sets out the rules of conduct for all road users and gives a summary of the law. The DSA also supervises professional driving instructors and is responsible for the compulsory basic training scheme for motor cyclists.

There are medical requirements that drivers must meet. These include an eyesight test; drivers must be able to read a clean car number plate at set distances. People suffering from certain conditions, such as epilepsy (unless controlled), disabling giddiness or fainting, would not normally be allowed a licence. In the case of certain disabilities a short-term or restricted licence may, however, be issued. Minimum ages for driving are:

—16 for riders of mopeds and disabled drivers of specially adapted vehicles;

—17 for drivers of cars and other passenger vehicles with nine or fewer seats (including that of the driver), motor cycles and goods vehicles not over 3·5 tonnes permissible maximum weight;

—18 for goods vehicles over 3·5 but not over 7·5 tonnes; and

—21 for passenger vehicles with over nine seats and goods vehicles over 7·5 tonnes.

A provisional licence costs £17, but can be exchanged free of charge for a full licence once the driving test has been passed. A full driving licence is valid until the age of 70, and thereafter has to be renewed at intervals of one or three years, dependent upon the driver's medical circumstances.

Before most new cars and goods vehicles are allowed on the roads, they are required to meet a number of safety and environmental requirements, based primarily on standards drawn up by the European Community. This form of control, known as type approval, is operated by the Vehicle Certification Agency.

The Secretary of State for Transport has a statutory responsibility for ensuring the roadworthiness of vehicles in use on the roads. The Vehicle Inspectorate is the national testing and enforcement authority. It meets this responsibility mainly through:

—annual testing and certification of heavy goods vehicles, buses and coaches;

—administration of the car and motor cycle testing scheme, under which vehicles are tested at private garages authorised as test stations; and

—means such as roadside checks and inspection of operators' premises.

In Northern Ireland private cars five or more years old are tested at official vehicle inspection centres.

Road Safety

Although Great Britain has one of the highest densities of road traffic in the world, it has a good record on road safety, with one of the lowest road accident death rates in the European Community. In 1991 some 4,500 people were killed on the roads (a fall of 13 per cent on the 1990 figure), 51,500 seriously injured and 254,700 slightly injured. This compares with nearly 8,000 deaths a year in the mid-1960s. A number of factors have contributed to the long-term decline in casualty rates, such as:

—advances in vehicle safety standards;

—improvements in roads;

—the introduction of legislation on seat belt wearing and drinking and driving; and

—developments in road safety training, education and publicity.

The Government's aim is to reduce road casualties by one-third by the end of the century, compared with the 1981–85 average. Priority is given to reducing casualties among vulnerable road-users (children, pedestrians, cyclists and motor cyclists and older road users), particularly in urban areas, where some 70 per cent of road accidents occur. Other areas for achieving lower casualties are improvements in highway design, better protection for vehicle occupants, encouraging the use of cycle helmets and measures to combat drinking and driving.

Speed Limits
Speed limits are in force on all public roads in Britain. These vary according to the type of road concerned. The limits for cars are 30 mph (48 km/h) in built-up areas, 60 mph (97 km/h) on single-carriageway roads in rural areas and 70 mph (113 km/h) on motorways and other dual carriageways. Other limits are in force for buses and coaches, cars towing caravans, and other types of vehicles. The Government has recently issued guidelines for local authorities which wish to impose 20 mph (32 km/h) limits in suitable areas.

Drink-driving

Alcohol is a major factor in causing road accidents. It is estimated that one-sixth of all fatalities occur in accidents where at least one driver or rider is over the legal limit for alcohol. However, the number of fatal accidents caused by drink-driving has been falling. It is estimated that, whereas in 1985 over 1,100 people were killed in alcohol-related road accidents, this had fallen to about 800 by 1990. Because of the danger posed by drinking and driving, there is a maximum permissible alcohol level for drivers, first introduced in the Road Safety Act 1967. The law currently imposes a limit of 35 microgrammes of alcohol per 100 millilitres of breath, and corresponding levels of alcohol in blood and urine. The police can demand a breath sample where a driver has been involved in an accident or moving traffic offence or where they have reasonable cause to believe that he or she has alcohol in the body. There are severe penalties for breaches, including mandatory disqualification from driving for at least a year, a heavy fine (currently up to £2,000), and the possibility of imprisonment for up to six months.

Seat Belts

Car seat belts help considerably in reducing injury and have long been required for front seats on all new cars in Britain. Their use has been compulsory for front-seat passengers since January 1983. Studies at a selected number of hospitals before and after the introduction of the legislation showed significant falls in the number of car occupant victims arriving at those hospitals. Since 1987 it has been obligatory for rear seats on new cars to be fitted with seat belts or child restraints. The wearing of belts in the rear seats of cars fitted with them has been compulsory since September 1989 for children and July 1991 for adults.

Education

The Government, through the Department of Transport, has a major programme of road safety publicity and education. Government road safety education covers a wide range of issues, including the older road user, drinking and driving, child road safety, pedestrian, cyclist and car passenger safety. All these campaigns, together with those on other aspects of transport safety, are brought together under the Department of Transport's 'Safety on the Move' campaign. The Scottish Office also produces road safety material through its Scottish Road Safety Campaign. The DSA is promoting a series of publications aimed at improving road safety.

The Royal Society for the Prevention of Accidents is a voluntary body which aims to reduce accidents; much of its work is concerned with road safety. It produces educational materials, all of which are developed and tested by teachers and undergo thorough evaluation in schools before publication. It has also instituted an annual award for good practice in road safety education. The motoring organisations, the Automobile Association (AA) and the Royal Automobile Club, contribute to road safety in various ways, for example by informing members about new road safety technology and encouraging good driving practice. Other bodies providing information about road safety include the British Institute of Traffic Education Research, the Child Accident Prevention Trust, the Cyclist Touring Club and the Pedestrian Association.

Road Traffic Act 1991

Several additional measures to improve road safety were introduced by the Road Traffic Act 1991, including:

—a new offence of dangerous driving;

—mandatory retesting of drivers convicted of the most serious driving offences;

—a new offence, in England and Wales, of causing danger, to deal with vandals who put lives at risk by damaging road signs or dropping objects onto roads;

—tougher measures to deal with drink-drive offenders;

—the use of new technology, such as remote-operated cameras and radar speed-detectors, to improve the detection of speeding and traffic-light offences; and

—new powers to prohibit dangerous vehicles.

The Transport Research Laboratory

The Transport Research Laboratory (TRL), which is an executive agency of the Department of Transport, provides the technical advice, based on research, which helps the Government set standards for highway and vehicle design and to formulate transport, environmental and road safety policies. Increasingly, the research is directed towards issues that arise in international negotiations—particularly within Europe, on topics such as the regulations which govern vehicle design. Through the Overseas Development Administration, the TRL also assists developing countries with research to help solve their particular road transport problems.

The TRL undertakes or manages much of the Department's expenditure on road research (£28 million in 1990–91). Nearly half this expenditure is on safety and environmental matters and most of the remainder is on highways, structures and traffic management issues.

The TRL is based on a 120-hectare (295-acre) site at Crowthorne in Berkshire, where it maintains an extensive range of facilities. These include a 3·8-km (2·4-mile) figure-of-eight test track which can be used for research on vehicle handling, skidding, spray reduction, noise and crash testing. A structures hall can test sections of bridges to breaking point under environmentally-controlled conditions and a £1·5 million test house carries out accelerated tests on road surfaces. These facilities, used in TRL research on structures and highways, help maximise value for money in spending on road construction and maintenance.

The programme on road safety includes research on the analysis of accident trends, the effects of alcohol and drugs, the nature and cost of injuries, public attitudes, driver training and the design of safer vehicles. Traffic research covers such matters as 20 mph zones, novel parking systems, improved junction designs and the development of information technology to help drivers make efficient and safe journeys.

Traffic in Towns

Traffic management schemes are used in many urban areas to reduce congestion, create a better environment and improve road safety. Such schemes include, for example:

—one-way streets;

—priority measures for public transport, such as bus lanes;

—facilities for pedestrians and cyclists; and

—traffic calming measures such as road humps or chicanes to constrain traffic speeds in residential areas.

Many towns have shopping precincts which are designed for the convenience of pedestrians and from which motor vehicles are excluded for all or part of the day. Controls over on-street parking

are enforced through excess charges and fixed penalties, supported where appropriate by powers to remove vehicles. In parts of London wheel clamping to immobilise illegally parked vehicles is also used. In December 1991 the Department of Transport published new guidance on traffic management measures to assist buses in urban areas, emphasising the need for co-operation between operators, local authorities and the police.

London

In London the Road Traffic Act 1991 makes provision for the designation of a network of priority 'red routes', which will be subject to special parking restrictions and other traffic management measures, strictly enforced with higher penalties. Monitoring of a pilot scheme in north and east London, introduced in January 1991, has shown significant falls in journey times and greater reliability for buses. In November 1991 a Traffic Director for London was appointed to ensure the coherent development and operation of the priority routes throughout London. The Act also provides new arrangements for more effective parking enforcement, giving London local authorities responsibility for enforcing controls. These arrangements will enable the police and traffic wardens to concentrate their efforts on the priority routes and other main roads.

London Transport (LT—see p. 21), which is responsible for bus transport in London, launched its London Bus Priority Initiative in July 1990. This involves co-operation with the Department of Transport, the police and the London boroughs. LT maintains a bus priority design team to work with those run by the individual boroughs. LT has also run a major publicity campaign to highlight the problem of congestion affecting the buses.

A computer-based traffic light optimisation system called 'Scoot' is also being introduced; some 250 junctions in London are fitted. Scoot minimises traffic delays by continuously adjusting signal timings over a network of junctions in response to traffic flows. As part of a wide-ranging government research programme into urban congestion, the possibility of road pricing is being examined. This would involve charging the car user for using certain roads or entering certain parts of a town by car. Such schemes would rely on modern technology to detect and recognise individual cars passing certain points, so that the owner can be billed accordingly.

Road Haulage

Road haulage traffic by heavy goods vehicles amounted to 130,600 million tonne-km in 1990, 1 per cent less than in 1989. There has been a move towards larger and more efficient vehicles carrying heavier loads—about 78 per cent of the traffic, in terms of tonne-km, is carried in vehicles of over 25 tonnes gross laden weight. Much of the traffic is moved over short distances, with 75 per cent of the tonnage being carried on hauls of 100 km (62 miles) or less. Public haulage—that is, private road hauliers carrying other firms' goods—accounts for 73 per cent of freight carried in Great Britain in terms of tonne-km. In 1990 the main commodities handled by heavy goods vehicles were:

—crude minerals (354 million tonnes);

—food, drink and tobacco (299 million tonnes); and

—building materials (178 million tonnes).

Road haulage is predominantly an industry of small, privately owned businesses. There were some 132,000 holders of an operator's licence in 1990. About half the heavy goods vehicles are in fleets of ten or fewer vehicles. The biggest operators in Great Britain are NFC plc (formerly the National Freight Consortium), Transport Development Group plc, TNT Express (UK) Ltd and United Carriers International Ltd.

Licensing and Other Controls

In general, those operating goods vehicles over 3·5 tonnes gross weight require an operator's licence. Licences are divided into restricted licences for own-account operators, carrying goods connected with their own business, and standard licences for hauliers operating for hire or reward. Proof of professional competence, financial standing and good repute is needed to obtain a standard licence. In Northern Ireland own-account operators do not require a licence. Regulations lay down limits on the hours worked by drivers of goods vehicles, as well as minimum rest periods. Tachographs, which automatically record speed, distance covered, driving time and stopping periods, must be fitted and used in most goods vehicles over 3·5 tonnes gross weight in Great Britain. The Government has announced a proposal to fit speed limiters to heavy lorries, preventing them from travelling above 60 mph (97 km/h).

International Road Haulage

International road haulage has grown rapidly and in 1990 1·4 million road goods vehicles were ferried to the continent of Europe or to the Irish Republic. Of these, 350,000 were powered vehicles registered in Britain. They carried over 9 million tonnes to and from continental Europe. The average length of haul by these vehicles was 1,170 km (727 miles) outwards and 1,100 km (684 miles) inwards, compared with 79 km (49 miles) for national road haulage. In addition, much traffic crossed the Irish land boundary.

International road haulage has been constrained by the need for permits issued under bilateral agreements with the 26 countries concerned. Many countries place no restriction on the number of British lorries which may enter them, but some agreements specify an annual quota of permits. Quotas of European Community permits are also available for international haulage or for cabotage (the operation of domestic road haulage services within a member state by a non-resident) anywhere within the Community. Full liberalisation of international road haulage within the Community without permits, except for cabotage, will apply from January 1993.

Passenger Services

Major changes in the structure of the passenger transport industry have occurred in recent years. Privatisation of the National Bus Company (which was the largest single bus and coach operator in Britain, operating through 72 subsidiaries in England and Wales) was completed in 1988. Each subsidiary was sold separately, and encouragement was given for a buy-out by the local management or employees. The privatisation of the Scottish Bus Group, previously the largest operator of bus services in Scotland with some 3,000 buses, as ten separate companies, was completed in 1991. Legislation has facilitated the privatisation of bus services run by municipal authorities.

London Transport (LT) is a statutory corporation, with its board members appointed by the Secretary of State for Transport. Within LT the main wholly-owned operating subsidiaries are London Underground Ltd and London Buses Ltd. Financial support—almost entirely for capital projects—is provided by central government. LT is required to involve the private sector in the provision of services where this is more efficient, and has been set objectives on safety, the quality of services and on its financial performance. Overall, London Buses Ltd, which operates through 11 subsidiary bus companies, runs 490 of London's 590 routes, many under direct contract to LT. It has some 5,000 buses. Many London bus routes are now run by private firms operating under contract to LT. A total of 223 routes have been put out for tender, of which 123 are run by London Buses Ltd and 100 are run by independent operators.

In Northern Ireland almost all road passenger services are provided by subsidiaries of the publicly owned Northern Ireland Transport Holding Company. Citybus Ltd operates services in the city of Belfast and Ulsterbus Ltd operates most of the services in the rest of Northern Ireland. These companies have some 300 and 1,000 vehicles respectively.

As well as the major bus operators, there are also a large number of small, privately-owned undertakings, often operating fewer than five vehicles. Double-deck buses are the main type of vehicle used for urban road passenger transport in Britain, with some 22,000 in operation. However, there has been a substantial increase in the number of minibuses and midibuses in recent years, with some 20,000 now in use. In addition, there are some 30,000 other single-deck buses and coaches.

Rural bus services are often supplemented by the so-called 'post bus', first tried in 1967. This is a minibus the prime purpose of which is to collect and deliver the mail but which also carries fare-paying passengers. By 1990 there were 145 post bus routes in Scotland, 26 in England and 12 in Wales.

Deregulation

Local bus services in Great Britain were deregulated in 1986, except in London. This means that bus operators are now able to run routes without needing a special licence. Instead, six weeks' notice of the introduction, variation or cancellation of a service has to be given to the appropriate traffic commissioner (one for each of the eight traffic areas of Great Britain). Local authorities can subsidise the provision of socially necessary services after competitive tendering.

Deregulation led to an increase of 19 per cent in local bus mileage outside London between 1985–86 and 1990–91, with some 84 per cent of services operated without subsidy in 1990–91. Over the same period the number of passengers has fallen by 19 per cent outside London, in line with long-term trends. Deregulation also had a noticeable effect during the 1980s on long-distance express coach services, bringing about reductions in fares, the provision of more services and an increase in passengers. The Government is proposing the deregulation of bus services in London and the privatisation of London Buses Ltd, for which legislation would be necessary. The earliest possible date for deregulation is 1994, with privatisation of London Buses Ltd subsidiaries taking place about a year later. A new London Bus Executive would be created to undertake certain functions which the market would have little incentive to provide or which would benefit from central co-ordination. Provision would be made for the operation of socially necessary but uneconomic services and for the continuation of a London-wide concessionary travel scheme.

Taxis

There are about 51,000 licensed taxis in Great Britain, mainly in urban areas; London has some 16,000. In London and a number of other cities taxis must be purpose-built to conform to very strict requirements and drivers must have passed a test of their knowledge of the area. Private hire vehicles with drivers ('minicabs') may be booked only through the operator and not hired on the street; in most areas outside London private hire vehicles are licensed. The Government is considering whether to introduce a licensing system for minicabs in London.

A local authority can refuse to grant a taxi licence only if it is satisfied that there is no unfulfilled demand for taxis in its area. Taxi operators are able to run regular local services and can tender in competition with bus operators for services subsidised by local authorities. To do this, they may apply for a special 'restricted' bus operator's licence, allowing them to run local services without having to obtain a full bus operator's licence. Taxis and licensed private hire vehicles may also offer shared rides to passengers paying separate fares.

In Northern Ireland there are some 4,000 licensed taxis. Licences are issued by the Department of the Environment for Northern Ireland on a basis broadly similar to that in Great Britain. Licensed taxis carry a public service vehicle disc on the windscreen, while the drivers are issued with an identity badge containing a licence number and photograph.

Railways

Origins of Britain's Railway System

Railways were pioneered in Britain. The world's first steam loco-motive, designed by Richard Trevethick (1771–1833), ran on the Penydarren tramway in south Wales in 1804; earlier tramways had relied on horse traction. The Penydarren engine was not particu-larly successful, being too heavy, but over the following 20 years engineers such as John Blenkinsop (1783–1831) and George Stephenson (1781–1848) built other, more serviceable, locomo-tives, generally for use on colliery railways intended to move coal to the quayside. A major step forward was the opening in 1825 of the Stockton and Darlington Railway. This was the first public passen-ger railway in the world to be worked by steam power, although it, too, also used horses. It was followed in 1830 by the opening of the Liverpool and Manchester Railway, which from the beginning was worked entirely by steam. This heralded an era of rapid railway building, which reached a climax in 1846 when no fewer than 270 Acts of Parliament for the construction of new railways were passed.

The railways brought cheap travel within reach of ordinary people's incomes. In 1844 the Railway Regulation Act stipulated that each company should run at least one train a day for a fare of not more than one penny a mile, the so-called 'parliamentary' trains. This helped ensure the role of the railways as the first mass transport system. Progress was rapid in increasing the speed of trains and in cutting journey times. The Victorians were also responsible for many of the feats of engineering still in use in Britain's railways, such as the Forth Bridge and the Severn Tunnel. The railway system continued to develop in speed, safety and comfort, with the introduction of ever more powerful locomotives and innovations such as vacuum brakes and corridor coaches. A new world speed record for steam locomotives, which still stands, was set when the engine *Mallard* reached a speed of 203 km/h (126 mph) in 1938.

The Government took a hand in the organisation of the railways with the 1923 grouping. Under this, the many existing railway companies were amalgamated into just four: the Great Western Railway, the London Midland and Scottish Railway, the London and North Eastern Railway and the Southern Railway. These companies remained in private hands until 1948, when the railway system was nationalised as British Railways. The 1950s and 1960s saw the progressive replacement of steam locomotives by diesels (a process complete by 1968), while major investment programmes included the electrification of the west coast main line.

The former British Rail Engineering Ltd, which built and overhauled rolling stock, was privatised as BREL in 1989. Other former parts of the railway operation have also been sold, including catering, hotels and ferries.

Current Organisation

The British Railways Board, set up in 1962, controls the British Rail (BR) network in Great Britain. It is organised into five business sectors:

—InterCity;

—Network SouthEast;

—Regional Railways;

—Railfreight Distribution; and

—Trainload Freight.

The first three of these operate passenger services, while the latter two are concerned with freight. In the seven metropolitan areas Regional Railways provides services under agreements with local government. In the English metropolitan regions (Greater Manchester, Merseyside, South Yorkshire, Tyne and Wear, West Midlands and West Yorkshire) the passenger transport authorities, composed of councillors nominated by district councils, decide fares and policies; their passenger transport executives secure the services from BR. In Scotland, the Strathclyde regional council operates as the passenger transport authority for its area.

A subsidiary company of BR, European Passenger Services Ltd, has been set up to operate international rail services through the Channel Tunnel (see p. 60). Other subsidiary businesses are:

—British Rail Maintenance Ltd, which is responsible for maintenance and light repair of British Rail rolling stock;

—Transmark, which provides consultancy services overseas on railway and associated operations; and

—BR Telecommunications, a new company marketing communications services.

BR is currently developing its sector structure further to devolve decision-making from headquarters. The aim is to make the sectors more responsive to customer requirements. Further measures to improve the service that BR gives to the travelling public are proposed in the Citizen's Charter. These include:

—refunds for passengers where trains were cancelled or unreasonably delayed;

—full refunds for passengers who decided not to travel because their train was cancelled;

—a scheme for discounts on renewal of annual season ticket holders to compensate them for poor service in the previous year; and

—reformed, easy-to-understand 'conditions of carriage' to replace the present ones.

The Government wishes to bring better services for all passengers as rapidly as possible. It considers that the franchising of services to the private sector provides the best way to achieve this. It is committed in the course of the present Parliament to:

—giving the private sector the fullest possible opportunity to operate existing services by means of franchising;

—the introduction of required standards of punctuality, reliability and quality of service in these franchises;

—the continuation where necessary of subsidy and the maintenance of through-ticketing;

—the appointment of an independent Rail Regulator, who would ensure that all companies have fair access to the track;

—the reorganisation of BR's internal structures into one part that will continue to be responsible for track and infrastructure and another that will operate passenger services until they are franchised out to the private sector; and

—the outright sale of BR's freight and parcels operations.

In Northern Ireland the Northern Ireland Railways Company Ltd, a subsidiary of the Northern Ireland Transport Holding Company, operates the railway service on some 320 km (200 miles) of track.

A £66·5 million programme to upgrade the Belfast to Dublin railway was announced in a joint statement by the British and Irish Governments in April 1992. The present line will be upgraded to permit speeds of 145 km/h (90 mph), which will shorten journeys by 15 to 20 minutes, and new signalling equipment and rolling stock will be provided. Expenditure on the Northern Ireland section will be about £24 million. The European Community has indicated that grant support of up to 75 per cent of the cost of the project will be provided.

British Rail Operations

In 1990–91 BR's turnover, including financial support and income from other activities but excluding internal transactions, was £3,777 million, of which £2,825 million was derived from rail passenger services and £682 million from freight services. It received grants of £602 million as compensation for the public service obligation to operate sections of the passenger network in the Regional sector and Network SouthEast which would not otherwise cover their cost.

BR has a substantial investment programme. Investment totalled £858 million in 1990–91 and is expected to rise to over £1,000 million in each of the next three years. Major areas of expenditure include:

—rolling stock and facilities for Channel Tunnel traffic from 1993 (see p. 62);

Table 5: Railway Operations

	1987 -88	1988 -89	1989 -90	1990 -91
Passenger journeys (million)	727	764	758	763
Passenger-km (million)	33,141	34,322	33,648	33,191
Freight traffic (million tonnes)	144	150	143	138
Trainload and wagonload traffic (million net-tonne km)	17,466	18,103	16,742	15,986
Assets at end of period:				
Locomotives	2,270	2,180	2,095	2,030
High Speed Train power units	197	197	197	197
Other coaching units	14,648	14,258	13,833	13,631
Freight vehicles[a]	28,884	24,922	21,970	20,763
Stations (including freight and parcels)	2,554	2,596	2,598	2,615
Route open for traffic (km)	16,633	16,598	16,588	16,584

Source: British Railways Board.

[a] In addition, a number of privately owned wagons and locomotives are operated on the railway network for customers of British Rail. Some 13,640 freight vehicles and 15 diesel locomotives were authorised for working on the network at the end of March 1991.

—new rolling stock and infrastructure improvements in Network SouthEast; and

—investment in new diesel multiple-unit trains in the Regional Railways sector.

At the end of March 1991, there were 105 locomotives and 1,216 coaches on order. Improvements are also being made to the track, for example, in 1990–91 some 220 km (138 miles) of track were relaid using continuous welded rail, which will reduce noise nuisance.

Safety remains a high priority, including the implementation of the safety recommendations of the inquiry into a major railway accident at Clapham Junction, south London, in December 1988. Investment in safety-related projects was about £140 million in 1990–91, and is scheduled to rise substantially. A comprehensive safety plan was published in February 1991, setting out the key initiatives being pursued to improve safety and laying down clear objectives. These include a safety management programme setting up regular safety meetings at all levels, correcting potentially unsafe conditions and developing training.

Passenger Services

The passenger network comprises a fast inter-city network, linking the main centres of Great Britain; local stopping services; and commuter services in and around the large conurbations, especially London and south-east England. BR runs over 700 InterCity expresses each weekday, serving about 90 business and leisure centres.

InterCity 125 trains, travelling at maximum sustained speeds of 125 mph (201 km/h), provide over 40 per cent of InterCity train mileage and are the world's fastest diesel trains. They operate from London:

—to the west of England and south Wales;

—to the East Midlands; and

—on cross-country services through the West Midlands, linking south-west England or south Wales with north-west England or north-east England and Edinburgh.

With the introduction of the new electric InterCity 225 trains, BR now has more trains running at over 160 km/h (100 mph) than any other railway.

About 28 per cent of route-mileage is electrified, including BR's busiest InterCity route, linking London, the West Midlands, the North West and Glasgow. The most recent major electrification scheme is that for the east coast main line between London and Edinburgh (including the line from Doncaster to Leeds). This scheme, covering some 644 km (400 miles) and costing £450 million at 1990–91 prices, commenced full passenger services between London King's Cross and Edinburgh in July 1991.

Many of the older electric multiple-units used for commuting services in London and south-east England are being replaced by more efficient rolling stock. The first of a new generation of 'Networker' trains is due to enter service in Kent in summer 1992. A diesel version is being brought into service on lines to the west of London, with 180 vehicles due to be delivered between 1992 and 1994. In the Regional sector, class 158 diesel multiple-units are replacing old locomotive-hauled stock on many long-distance routes.

New lines are being introduced to the network. Three major new rail links to airports have been built or are planned:

—a new link between Stansted airport and London Liverpool Street, which was opened in January 1991;

—a link to connect Manchester airport to the Manchester to Wilmslow (Cheshire) line, currently under construction; and

—a joint venture with BAA plc for a £235 million project (to be financed largely by BAA) between Heathrow airport and London Paddington.

New stations are being built, and some former stations are being reopened. Changes in demand, for example caused by new housing developments, can sometimes be the trigger for such investment. In 1990–91, 17 stations were opened or reopened.

Freight

Over 90 per cent of rail freight traffic is of bulk commodities, mainly coal, coke, iron and steel, building materials and petroleum.

Intermodal services are being developed to give easy transfer of loads between road and rail vehicles. Railfreight is a partner in Charterail, a joint venture with the private sector using intermodal technology to enter domestic distribution markets currently using road-only services.

The opening of the Channel Tunnel will present an important opportunity for non-bulk freight movement. Freight routes in Kent and Sussex are being upgraded in preparation for the traffic, and new locomotives are being purchased. Container traffic to the continent of Europe and further afield is being developed and new container-carrying wagons have been ordered.

Table 6: Freight Commodities carried by Rail 1980-90

Million tonnes	1980	1985[a]	1990
Coal and coke	94·1	65·9	74·9
Metals	13·0	14·1	18·4
Construction materials	15·9	16·6	21·9
Other	30·5	25·4	25·9
Total	153·5	122·0	141·1

Source: Department of Transport.
[a] Carryings of coal and coke in 1985 were reduced by the miners' dispute.

Railways in London

London has had an underground railway system since the mid-nineteenth century, when the first lines were dug. Early lines included the Metropolitan, first opened in 1863, and the District, first opened in 1868. These were built on the 'cut-and-cover' method, and initially used steam engines. The earliest of the deep-level 'tubes' was the Northern Line, the first stretch of which opened in 1890. This used electric traction from the start, which soon superseded steam elsewhere on the system. The network has continued to expand since, with new lines such as the Victoria Line, completed in 1971, and with extensions to existing lines. Today London Underground Ltd operates services on 394 km (245 miles) of railway, of which about 169 km (105 miles) are underground. The system has 273 stations, with 478 trains operating in the peak period. Some 775 million passenger journeys were made on London Underground trains in 1990–91, with some 53·6 million train-km (33·3 million train-miles) being run.

Major investment in the Underground is being undertaken. Plans to expand the network include:

—an extension of the Jubilee Line to Stratford (east London) via Docklands and the north Greenwich peninsula, expected to open in 1996 and costing about £1,500 million at 1990 prices;

—the £1,700 million CrossRail linking Paddington with Liverpool Street, intended to open around the turn of the century, the tunnel of which would be used by British Rail as well as Underground trains; and

—the proposed Chelsea-Hackney line, a new tunnel linking the Wimbledon branch of the District line to a branch of the Central line, costing £1,800 million at 1990 prices.

Further plans for the extension of the network are also under consideration.

London Underground is undertaking a large programme to improve the safety and quality of the existing system. Safety will continue to be the main priority—by the year 2000 London Underground will have spent more than £1,000 million on improving safety. London Underground's total investment programme in 1990–91 was a record £459 million. Major projects provided for in the following three years include a £750 million modernisation of the Central line and the total reconstruction of the Angel Station.

Also part of London's transport system is the Docklands Light Railway (DLR), which first opened in 1987 and makes use for part of its length of former railway lines. Ownership of the DLR is being transferred from LT to the London Docklands Development Corporation. The DLR is being upgraded and extended; a total of £139 million was invested in the system in 1990–91. New, larger trains are being introduced to accommodate more people. An extension westward to the City of London opened in July 1991, and another eastward to Beckton is due to open at the end of 1992. A further extension to Lewisham in south London via a tunnel under the River Thames has been approved by Parliament. At the end of 1991, the DLR served 16 stations and operated services on 14 km (8·5 miles) of track.

BR operates two underground lines in London, from Waterloo to Bank stations and from Moorgate to Finsbury Park. A light railway network for Croydon and the surrounding area of south London is being taken forward by LT and the London Borough of Croydon.

Other Urban Railways

At present, there are few other urban railway systems in Great Britain. Existing ones include the Glasgow Underground and the Tyne and Wear Metro, a 59-km (37-mile) light rapid transit system with 46 stations first opened in 1980.

However, several schemes have been put forward in recent years, and some are coming to fruition. The initial section of the Manchester Metrolink project, designed, built and operated by GMML, a private sector consortium, opened in April 1992. The first stage, which when completed will cover some 31 km (19 miles), will link Manchester's main railway termini and provide improved services to Bury and Altrincham as a result of conversion of existing BR services to light rapid transit. Other routes are planned or under consideration.

In Sheffield, the construction of a 30-km (18-mile) light railway was started in September 1991. The 'Supertram' network is due for completion in 1995, with the first stage opening in 1993. For roughly half its length, the line will run in the streets, with most of the other half consisting of segregated track running alongside roads. A short length of BR track will also be converted to the tram system. The total cost of the system will be some £230 million, making it the largest local public transport scheme to be approved outside London for nearly 20 years.

In the West Midlands work is planned on another major light rail project, Midland Metro. Its first line, from Birmingham to Wolverhampton, has been approved by Parliament. Most of the route follows a disused railway, with some on-street running. It will be built and operated by the private sector, with capital costs assisted by the Department of Transport. Private Bills for two further routes were deposited in Parliament in 1989.

Light rapid transit systems are also being considered in a number of other towns and cities, including Bristol, Edinburgh, Glasgow and Southampton.

Private Railways

There are over 70 small, privately owned passenger-carrying railways in Great Britain. Most of these are operated on a voluntary basis and provide limited services for tourists and railway enthusiasts. The main aim of most of these railways is the preservation and operation of steam locomotives. They are generally run on former British Rail branch lines reopened as preserved steam railways.

There are also several narrow-gauge lines, mainly in north Wales. Many of these were originally built to transport slate away from the quarries, but also took passengers. Following the demise of the slate industry, the railways remain as considerable tourist attractions in their own right. Small railways in England include

the Ravenglass and Eskdale Railway in Cumbria and the Romney, Hythe and Dymchurch Railway in Kent, both laid at the very narrow 15 in (38.1 cm) gauge. The latter is the longest and most fully equipped 15 in gauge railway in the world.

An unusual narrow-gauge railway is Mail Rail, the Post Office's underground railway line through London. First opened in 1927, it covers 10 km (6 miles) from Paddington station, through several of the major sorting offices in central London, to Whitechapel. Its trains run on a 2 foot (60.96 cm) gauge line.

Inland Waterways

The inland waterways of Great Britain are popular for recreation, make a valuable contribution to the quality of the environment, play an important part in land drainage and water supply, and are used to a limited extent for freight-carrying. The publicly owned British Waterways Board (BWB) is responsible for some 3,200 km (2,000 miles) of waterways in Great Britain. It owns 60 tunnels, nearly 400 aqueducts, over 1,500 locks, 2,000 heritage structures and 57 Sites of Special Scientific Interest. The BWB is taking steps to develop its business more commercially with greater responsiveness to market needs and waterway users. In 1990–91 the BWB's turnover amounted to £27·1 million and it received a government grant of £49·7 million to maintain its waterways to statutory standards.

The majority of waterways are used primarily for recreation and leisure, but about 620 km (385 miles) are maintained as commercial waterways. An official survey of inland waterway freight traffic found that in 1990, 69 million tonnes of freight were carried on inland waterways and estuaries, amounting to some 2,400 million tonne-km moved.

Leisure use of Britain's waterways is considerable—some 25,000 pleasure boats use BWB waterways alone. Over 1 million people travel on its waterways each year for boating holidays, floating restaurant trips or some other form of relaxation. In addition, some 6 million people visit the BWB's canals for informal recreation and over 800,000 anglers fish in their waters. The BWB is developing much of its historic canalside property for recreational and commercial use, often in conjunction with the private sector. Canal restoration programmes, often undertaken with the assistance of volunteers, mean that more waterways are becoming available for such purposes. In 1990 the BWB-owned Kennet and Avon canal reopened after being closed for almost 40 years, and in May 1991 51 km (32 miles) of the privately-owned Basingstoke Canal were reopened. These projects were largely financed by the local authorities through whose areas the canals pass, and they are contributing to their upkeep. Overall, since the mid-1970s the BWB has restored about 300 km (200 miles) of its waterways to navigable standards.

Shipping and Ports

As an island nation, Britain has a long maritime tradition and has depended on the sea for its trade since its earliest history. Archaeologists have discovered remains of this activity, excavating, for example, Roman and medieval wharves in the City of London, which was a great centre for trade with many parts of Europe. British mariners also played a part in the great era of exploration in the fifteenth century onwards: John Cabot, for example, sailed from Bristol on his expeditions to Newfoundland and Greenland. The Honourable East India Company was founded in 1600 to conduct trade to India and the Far East. For well over 200 years their ships sailed eastwards, laying the foundations of British influence in India. In the seventeenth to nineteenth centuries, a large merchant fleet came into being, and British vessels traded virtually all over the world.

In the nineteenth century British merchant shipping faced considerable competition at sea, particularly from the United States. However, by the beginning of the twentieth century, the British shipping industry had achieved a dominant position—the British merchant fleet in 1914 amounted to 42 per cent of the world fleet. British merchant seamen gave courageous service in both World Wars, and the merchant service was granted the title of Merchant Navy by King George V in recognition of the hazards it had shared with the Royal Navy during the Great War.

Present Shipping

In September 1991 British companies owned 791 trading vessels of 14·8 million deadweight tonnes. These included 202 vessels totalling 9·0 million deadweight tonnes used as oil, liquid chemical or gas carriers and 559 vessels totalling 5·7 million deadweight tonnes employed as dry bulk carriers, container ships or other types of cargo ships. Some 80 per cent of British-owned vessels are registered in Britain or British dependent territories such as Bermuda.

The tonnage of the British registered trading fleet has been declining in recent years. To help address this, and in response to the 1990 report of a joint government and shipping industry working party, the Government has simplified technical procedures and regulations governing ship registration requirements. The Government also has work in hand designed to:

—introduce flexibility into the rules governing the nationality of officers on British ships;

—allow chartered vessels to be registered in Britain; and

—secure the liberalisation of cabotage and a more competitive financial environment.

The Government also makes funds available for Merchant Navy officer training, the repatriation of crews in the deep-sea trades and to support a Reserve of ex-seafarers willing to serve in the Merchant Navy in an emergency.

Cargo Services

About 94 per cent by weight (76 per cent by value) of Britain's overseas trade is carried by sea. In 1990 British seaborne trade amounted to 300 million tonnes (valued at £173,000 million) or 1,153,000 million tonne-km (716,500 million tonne-miles). British registered ships carried 18 per cent by weight and 34 per cent by value. Tanker cargo accounted for 45 per cent of this trade by weight, but only 8 per cent by value; foodstuffs and manufactured goods accounted for 88 per cent by value.

Virtually all the scheduled cargo liner services from Britain are containerised. The British tonnage serving these trades is dominated by a relatively small number of private sector companies and, in deep sea trades, they usually operate in conjunction with other companies on the same routes in organisations known as 'conferences'. The object of these groupings is to ensure regular and efficient services with stable freight rates, to the benefit of both shipper and shipowner. In addition to the carriage of freight by liner and bulk services between Britain and Europe, there are many roll-on, roll-off services to carry cars, passengers and commercial vehicles.

Passenger Services

In 1990 there were 30 million international sea passenger movements between Britain and the rest of the world, compared with 74 million international air movements in 1989. Almost all the passengers who arrived at or departed from British ports in 1990 travelled to or from the continent of Europe or the Irish Republic. In 1990 some 79,000 passengers embarked on pleasure cruises from British ports.

Traffic from the southern and south-eastern ports accounts for a substantial proportion of traffic to the continent of Europe. The main British operators are Sealink Stena Line, P&O and Hoverspeed, although not all of their vessels are under the British flag. Services are provided by roll-on roll-off ferries, hovercraft, hydrofoils and high-speed catamarans.

Domestic passenger and freight ferry services also run to many of the offshore islands, such as the Isle of Wight, the Orkney and Shetland Islands, and the islands off the west coast of Scotland. It is estimated that in 1989 there were some 45 million passenger movements on such internal services.

Merchant Shipping Legislation and Policy

The Government's policy is one of minimum intervention and the encouragement of free and fair competition. However, regulations, administered by the Department of Transport, provide for marine safety and welfare, the investigation of accidents and the prevention of and cleaning up of pollution from ships. The Government also has certain reserve powers for protecting shipping and trading interests from measures adopted or proposed by overseas governments.

The Government also plays an important role in the formulation of shipping policy within the European Community. The first stage of a common shipping policy involved agreement in 1986 to regulations designed to:

—liberalise the Community's international trade;

—establish a competitive regime for shipping; and

—enable the Community to take action to combat protectionism from other countries and to counter unfair pricing practices.

For the second stage, now under consideration, a range of measures has been proposed to harmonise operating conditions and strengthen the competitiveness of Community members' merchant fleets. One such measure, facilitating the transfer of ships between member states' registers, has already been agreed. Of particular interest to Britain is a proposal to liberalise coastal shipping throughout the European Community.

Britain's longest 'cast-and-push bridge' nears completion. Crossing the River Ceiriog in north Wales, it comprises a prestressed concrete box girder deck supported on concrete piers. Temporary steel piers were used to support the deck during construction. This procedure is significantly cheaper than conventional methods.

Many of London's bus routes have been put out to competitive tender by London Transport, and some of them have been awarded to outside contractors, such as this number 24 operated by Grey-Green.

Motorways and major trunk roads

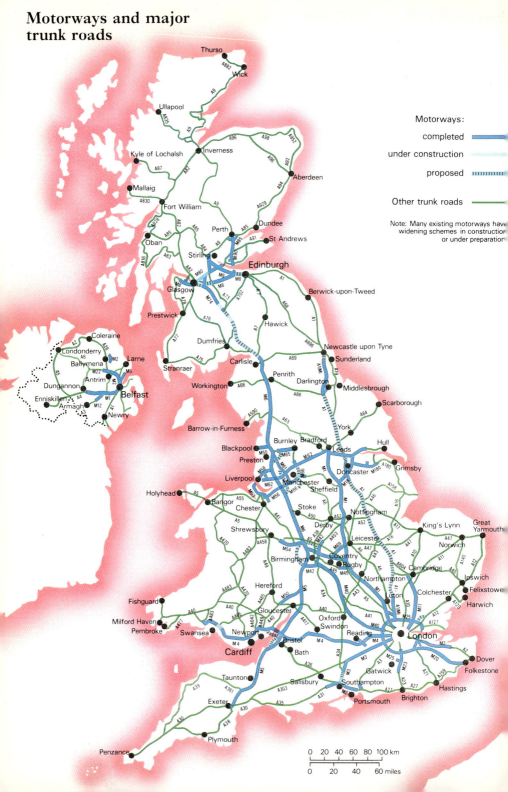

Motorways:

completed

under construction

proposed

Other trunk roads

Note: Many existing motorways have
widening schemes in construction
or under preparation

Thurso
Wick
A882
Ullapool
A9
A835
A96
A98
A952
Kyle of Lochalsh
Inverness
A87
A82
A96
A92
Aberdeen
Mallaig
A830
A9
A93
A929
Fort William
A828
A82
Dundee
Perth
A85
A91
Oban
A828
A85
St Andrews
A816
A83
Stirling
A84
A9
M90
Edinburgh
A82
M80
M9
A1
M8
Glasgow
M8
A8
Berwick-upon-Tweed
M77
A702
M74
A73
A7
Prestwick
A76
A68
Hawick
A77
Dumfries
A7
Newcastle upon Tyne
Coleraine
A2
Londonderry
A6
Ballymena
Larne
A696
Sunderland
Dungannon
Antrim
M5
A69
A1(M)
A19
Enniskillen
A4
M1
Stranraer
Carlisle
Penrith
Darlington
Middlesbrough
Armagh
M12
A3
Newry
Workington
A66
A66
Scarborough
A590
M6
A64
Barrow-in-Furness
A65
York
Blackpool
Burnley Bradford
Hull
Preston
M55
M65
M62
Leeds
Liverpool
M58
M61
Doncaster
M180
Grimsby
M62
Manchester
M1
Sheffield
A158
Holyhead
A5
M56
A1
A16
Bangor
A55
Stoke
A6
Chester
A50
Nottingham
Shrewsbury
A5
Derby
A52
A77
King's Lynn
Great Yarmouth
A483
A458
M54
A453
Leicester
A16
A47
Norwich
Birmingham
A40
M6
M69
A47
A604
Cambridge
A12
Ipswich
Hereford
M42
Coventry
M45
Rugby
Northampton
M1
Colchester
Felixstowe
A465
M50
A34
M40
A43
A5
Luton
Harwich
Fishguard
A40
A417
Oxford
A41
M25
Milford Haven
A40
A48
Gloucester
A40
Swindon
M40
A12
A127
Pembroke
Swansea
A449
Newport
A417
Reading
London
A477
M4
Bristol
M4
M4
A2
Cardiff
Bath
M3
M25
M20
Dover
A36
M3
A21
A259
Folkestone
Taunton
M5
Salisbury
Gatwick
A23
A27
Hastings
A319
A303
Southampton
M27
Exeter
A31
Brighton
A30
A361
Portsmouth
A38
Plymouth
Penzance
A30

0 20 40 60 80 100 km

0   20   40   60 miles

Main Railway Passenger Routes

Electrified InterCity
and Express Routes

Other InterCity
and Express Routes

Other routes

Note: Cambridge to King's Lynn,
electrified from August 1992.

Inverness

Aberdeen

Dundee

Perth

Stirling

Glasgow

Edinburgh

Berwick

Newcastleupon Tyne

Londonderry

Larne

Belfast

Carlisle

Darlington

Middlesborough

Scarborough

Harrogate

York

Leeds

Hull

Blackpool

Bradford

Preston

Manchester

Doncaster

Grimsby

Liverpool

Sheffield

Holyhead

Nottingham

Crewe

Derby

Stafford

King's Lynn

Shrewsbury

Leicester

Peterborough

Norwich

Birmingham

Coventry

Worcester

Cambridge

Ipswich

Hereford

Colchester

Harwich

Fishguard

Gloucester

Oxford

London

Swansea

Newport

Swindon

Margate

Cardiff

Bristol

Bath

Reading

Ashford

Dover

Gatwick

Folkestone

Taunton

Salisbury

Hastings

Southampton

Portsmouth

Brighton

Eastbourne

Exeter

Weymouth

Bournemouth

Newton Abbot

Penzance

Plymouth

0 20 40 60 80 100 km

0   20   40   60 miles

British Rail's new InterCity 225 trains have been introduced on the recently-electrified London-Edinburgh east coast main line. The InterCity 225 is designed to travel at speeds of 225 km/h.

A very different sort of train carries letters below London's streets. Mail Rail trains carry more than 10 million bags of mail a year between seven stations on their 37 km of track. The automatically-controlled electric trains provide a frequent service—up to one each way every four minutes at peak times.

Old and new parts of Britain's transport system meet—an aqueduct has been built to carry the Grand Union Canal over a new motorway. The prestressed concrete structure, some 120 metres long, is the first new aqueduct to be built on the London-Birmingham canal for half a century.

The Manchester Ship Canal, first opened for traffic in 1894, remains important for transporting goods such as chemicals, oil and timber. Manchester Port, the operator of the seaway that links the River Mersey to central Manchester, has recently completed the first stage of a £26 million programme to modernise its locks, bridges and sluices. Docks in Manchester or lower down the canal handle about 8 million tonnes of cargo a year.

British Airways operates nine of these British Aerospace 748s among their 240-strong aircraft fleet. The 748 provides services to the Scottish islands, flying between mainland cities such as Glasgow and Inverness and island destinations such as Shetland and Stornoway.

This fully-automated freight handling system enables one man to position pallets and containers speedily on a lorry as they are unloaded from an aeroplane. It is able to handle all sizes and shapes of freight containers. Following its success with British Airways, several overseas airlines are now using the system.

Construction work in progress on the Channel Tunnel. Britain is now physically linked to the continent of Europe for the first time since the Ice Age, following the link-up of the two halves of the Channel Tunnel in December 1990.

Dover is the world's busiest passenger port, with a ferry moving in or out of harbour every six minutes on average. A new vessel traffic management system has been installed to ensure safe and efficient operation. These consoles display information on all radar contacts from large ferries down to windsurfers, allowing the port control officers to pass on accurate information to mariners and shore-based personnel.

Like the mailcoaches of old, post buses carry passengers as well as mail. By 1990 there were over 180 routes in Great Britain providing rural communities with public transport.

The BT Worldwide Network Management Centre, recently opened in Oswestry, can locate trouble spots in the company's inland and international networks. The video wall in front of the control consoles, at 25 metres the longest in Europe, gives rapidly updated information on the state of the networks, allowing the network managers to take immediate action to prevent congestion.

Ports

There are about 80 ports of commercial significance in Great Britain, and in addition there are several hundred small harbours which cater for local cargoes, fisheries, island ferries and recreation. Harbour authorities, created by local Acts of Parliament, are of three main types—companies, local authorities and *ad hoc* public bodies known as trust port authorities. Within statutory ports' territorial limits, there are many privately-owned terminals.

Most of the company ports were originally developed by railway undertakings. The former British Transport Docks Board was privatised in 1981 as Associated British Ports Holdings PLC. This owns about a quarter of the industry, including Southampton and most of the south Wales and Humber ports. Its turnover totalled £176 million in 1990. British Rail passenger ferry ports, including Newhaven, Holyhead, Stranraer and Parkeston Quay (Harwich) were privatised in 1983. Other major company ports are Felixstowe, Liverpool (a trust port until 1971) and Manchester.

Trust port authorities manage many major ports, including Aberdeen, Dover, Ipswich, London, Milford Haven, Poole and Tyne. The Ports Act 1991 enables them to make schemes of conversion into companies. The first trust ports with such schemes are Clyde, Tees and Hartlepool, Medway and Forth. The Port of London Authority is selling its dock undertaking at Tilbury.

The local authority sector is the smallest, but includes the oil ports in Orkney and Shetland and also Portsmouth, a major ferry port. Another large municipal port, Bristol, was leased to a company in 1991.

Port Traffic

In 1990 traffic through the ports of Great Britain amounted to 475 million tonnes, comprising 136 million tonnes of exports, 180 million tonnes of imports and 160 million tonnes of domestic traffic (which included offshore traffic and landings of sea-dredged aggregates). About 53 per cent of the traffic was in fuels, mainly petroleum and petroleum products. Traffic through Northern Ireland ports totalled 17 million tonnes.

Table 7: Traffic through the Principal Ports of Great Britain[1] *million tonnes*

	1975	1985	1986	1987	1988	1989	1990
London	50·3	51·6	53·6	48·9	53·7	54·0	58·1
Tees and Hartlepool	20·2	30·6	30·7	33·9	37·4	39·3	40·2
Grimsby and Immingham	22·0	29·1	32·0	32·2	35·0	38·1	39·4
Sullom Voe	–	59·0	57·2	50·0	50·6	40·7	36·0
Milford Haven	44·9	32·4	30·0	32·7	33·3	33·0	32·2
Southampton	25·3	25·2	25·7	27·2	31·4	26·1	28·8
Forth	8·4	29·1	28·8	30·0	29·0	22·9	25·4
Liverpool	23·4	10·4	10·7	10·2	19·6	20·2	23·2
Felixstowe	4·1	10·1	10·8	13·3	15·6	16·5	16·4
Medway	21·7	10·4	10·4	11·6	12·7	14·0	13·6
Dover	3·7	9·3	9·9	10·6	10·4	13·5	13·0

Source: Department of Transport.
[1] Belfast and Larne are the main ports in Northern Ireland and handled 8 million tonnes and 4 million tonnes respectively in 1990.

The traffic handled by Britain's main ports, in terms of total tonnage handled, is set out in Table 7. Sullom Voe (Shetland), Milford Haven and Forth mostly handle oil, while the main ports for non-fuel traffic are London, Tees and Hartlepool, Grimsby and Immingham, Felixstowe and Dover. Ports on the south and east coasts have gained traffic at the expense of those on the west coast as the emphasis of Britain's trade has switched towards the continent of Europe, and with the worldwide switch from conventional handling methods to container and roll-on roll-off traffic.

Container and roll-on, roll-off traffic in Great Britain has almost trebled since 1975 to 87 million tonnes in 1990 and now accounts for about 72 per cent of non-bulk traffic. The leading ports for unitised traffic are Felixstowe, which handled 1·2 million units (chiefly containers) in 1990, Dover, which handled 1 million units (mainly road goods vehicles and trailers on roll-on roll-off ferries) and London, which handled 541,000 units, a mix of containers and vehicles on roll-on, roll-off ships.

Development

Most recent major port developments have been on the east and south coasts. A £50 million extension at Felixstowe and the new £100 million Thamesport terminal on the Medway cater for deep-sea container traffic. Growing roll-on, roll-off and container trade has led to expansion at Dartford, Dover, Portsmouth, Poole, Teesport, Hull and Immingham, and also at ports serving Ireland. Investment in bulk handling is in progress or planned on the Humber and the Medway.

Another long-term focus of investment has been the oil trade, notably at Southampton and Milford Haven and on the Thames and Mersey. Ports on the Forth and Tees gained from the development of oilfields in the British sector of the North Sea. Other terminals were built at Flotta in the Orkneys and Sullom Voe in the Shetlands (one of the largest in the world). Supply bases for offshore oil and gas installations were set up at a number of ports, notably Aberdeen, Great Yarmouth and Heysham.

Safety at Sea

HM Coastguard Service, part of the Department of Transport, is responsible for co-ordinating civil maritime search and rescue operations around the coastline of Britain. In a maritime emergency the Coastguard calls on and co-ordinates facilities such as:

—coastguard helicopters and cliff search and rescue companies;

—lifeboats of the Royal National Lifeboat Institution, a voluntary body which operates 268 lifeboats;

—Ministry of Defence aircraft, helicopters and ships; and

—merchant shipping and commercial aircraft.

In 1990 the Coastguard Service co-ordinated action in some 7,100 incidents (including cliff rescues), in which 13,500 people were assisted.

Compliance with rules of behaviour when navigating in traffic separation schemes around the shores of Britain is mandatory for all vessels of countries party to the Convention on the International Regulations for Preventing Collisions at Sea 1972. The most ıortant scheme affecting British waters is in the Dover Strait, world's busiest seaway. Britain and France jointly operate the nel Navigation Information Service, which provides navigational information and also monitors the movement of vessels in the strait.

The lighthouse authorities, which between them control about 370 lighthouses and many minor lights and buoys, are:

—the Corporation of Trinity House, which covers England and Wales;

—the Northern Lighthouse Board, for Scotland and the Isle of Man; and

—the Commissioners of Irish Lights for Ireland.

Responsibility for pilotage rests with harbour authorities under the Pilotage Act 1987.

In general, British shipping has a good safety record. However, following the loss of the *Herald of Free Enterprise* off Zeebrugge in 1987 with 189 lives confirmed lost, measures were introduced to improve the safety of roll-on roll-off ferries. These included a duty on shipowners to ensure the safe operation of their vessels, as well as a wide range of technical measures. Most of the action taken by Britain has been incorporated in the relevant international maritime safety conventions. The Government has also implemented most of the safety recommendations relating to passenger vessels on the Thames in the Marine Accident Investigation Branch report into the sinking of the pleasureboat *Marchioness* in 1989; it is intended that the remaining recommendations will be implemented during 1992.

Civil Aviation

The demands of passengers, both domestic and international, are responded to by an innovative British air transport industry. Airlines are seeking opportunities for modernisation, and this is complemented by the work of the aviation authorities in negotiating new international rights and improving facilities such as air traffic control. British airlines are entirely in the private sector.

Government Policy

The Secretary of State for Transport is responsible for aviation matters, including:

—negotiation of air service agreements with more than 100 other countries;

—the control of air services into Britain by overseas airlines;

—British participation in the activities of international aviation bodies;

—aviation security policy;

—amenity matters, such as aircraft noise and other environmental matters;

—investigation of accidents; and

—airports policy.

The Government's civil aviation policy aims to maintain high standards of safety and security and to achieve environmental improvements through reduced noise and other emissions from aircraft. It is concerned to promote the interests of travellers by encouraging a competitive British industry. The Government has taken the lead in the European Community and with bilateral partners in negotiating freer arrangements within which airline competition can flourish. New arrangements with an increasing number of countries are resulting in better provision of services at more competitive fares.

Civil Aviation Authority

The Civil Aviation Authority (CAA) is an independent statutory body, responsible for the economic and safety regulation of the industry and, jointly with the Ministry of Defence, for the provision of air navigation services. The CAA's primary objectives are to ensure that British airlines provide air services to satisfy all substantial categories of public demand at the lowest charges consistent with a high standard of safety and to further the reasonable interests of air transport users.

Air Traffic

Britain accounts for a large share of air transport within the European Community. Over half the international air passengers travelling between European Community countries started or ended at British airports, as did almost a third of those travelling between the European Community and the rest of the world.

Total capacity offered on all services by British airlines amounted to 20,199 million available tonne-km in 1990: 15,274 million tonne-km on scheduled services and 4,925 million tonne-km on non-scheduled services. The airlines carried 38·4 million passengers on scheduled services and 21·6 million on charter flights; some 76·4 million international terminal passengers travelled to or from Britain, a 3 per cent increase on 1989.

Table 8: Traffic at British Airports 1980–90

Air transport movements, thousands

	1980	1985	1990
International			
— British operators	320	367	479
— foreign operators	187	212	340
Domestic			
— British operators	223	260	301

Source: Department of Transport.

The value of Britain's overseas trade carried by air was some £43,467 million in 1990—20 per cent of the value of exports and 18 per cent of imports. Air freight is important for the carriage of goods with a high value-to-weight ratio, especially where speed of movement is essential.

British Airways

British Airways plc is one of the world's leading airlines. In terms of international scheduled services it is the largest in the world. During 1991 British Airways' turnover was £4,937 million (including £4,834 million from airline operations), and the British Airways group carried 25·6 million passengers on scheduled and charter flights both domestically and internationally. Previously state-owned, British Airways was privatised in 1987.

The British Airways scheduled route network, one of the largest in the world, serves 153 destinations in 69 countries. Its main operating base is London's Heathrow airport, but services from Gatwick and regional centres such as Manchester and Birmingham have been expanding. Scheduled Concorde supersonic services are operated from London Heathrow to New York, Washington and, in the summer, Toronto, crossing the Atlantic in about half the time taken by subsonic aircraft. In October 1991 British Airways had a fleet of 240 aircraft, the largest fleet in Western Europe, comprising 7 Concordes, 50 Boeing 747s, 8 McDonnell-Douglas DC10s, 13 Lockheed TriStars, 39 Boeing 757s, 10 Airbus A320s, 51 Boeing 737s, 13 Boeing 767s, 31 BAC One-Elevens, 9 British Aerospace Advanced Turboprops and 9 British Aerospace 748s. A total of 89 aircraft were on firm order. The average age of the fleet, at 9·8 years, is two years younger than the industry average.

Other Airlines

About 460 aircraft are operated by other airlines. Dan-Air Services is a major operator of both scheduled and charter services, and had a fleet of 40 aircraft in 1991. Virgin Atlantic operates out of Heathrow and Gatwick and flies scheduled services to New York, Los Angeles, Miami, Boston and Tokyo. It has seven Boeing 747 aircraft. British Midland and Air UK are both major domestic airlines and also operate a number of international and charter services.

Britannia Airways carried over 7 million passengers in 1990 and is one of the largest charter operators in the world. It has charter flights from 20 British airports to more than 100 destinations in

Europe and elsewhere, mostly operated for its associated company Thomson Holidays. It has 41 aircraft.

Helicopters and Other Aerial Work

Helicopters are engaged on a variety of work, especially operations connected with Britain's offshore oil and gas industry. The three main operators in Britain are Bristow Helicopters, Bond Helicopters and British International Helicopters, with 65, 45 and 27 helicopters respectively in 1990. Light aircraft and helicopters are also involved in other activities, such as charter operations, search and rescue services, medical evacuation, crop-spraying, aerial survey and photography, and police operations.

Air Safety

Britain has a good record in air safety; there were no fatal accidents at all involving British-registered fixed wing public transport aircraft in the 1990–91 financial year, the first time since records began. The CAA is responsible for both technical and operational air safety. Its Safety Regulation Group deals with the development and application of safety requirements for all civil aviation operations. It licenses flight crew, ground engineers and air traffic control officers, as well as aerodromes and fire and rescue services. Training of air traffic controllers is also provided by the CAA.

Every company operating aircraft used for commercial purposes must possess an Air Operator's Certificate, which is granted by the CAA when it is satisfied that the operator is competent to secure the safe operation of its aircraft. The CAA's flight operations inspectors, all of whom are experienced airline pilots, and airworthiness surveyors check that satisfactory standards are maintained.

Each member of the flight crew of a British-registered aircraft and every licensed ground engineer must hold the appropriate official licence issued by the CAA. Except for those with acceptable military or other qualifying experience, all applicants for a first professional licence must have undertaken a full-time course of instruction which has been approved by the CAA.

The European Community is increasingly involved in air safety matters. It is envisaged that in future common safety standards will apply throughout the Community. The CAA is therefore working towards the formulation of these common standards through the forum of the European Joint Aviation authorities, consisting of 19 countries.

Air Traffic Control and Navigation Services
Responsibility for civil and military air traffic control over Britain and the surrounding seas rests with the National Air Traffic Services (NATS), jointly operated by the CAA and the Ministry of Defence. At 13 civil aerodromes, including most of the major British airports, the NATS provides the navigation services necessary for aircraft taking off and landing, and integrates them into the flow of traffic within British airspace. Civil controllers at airports alone handled 1·6 million aircraft movements in 1990–91.

Britain plays a major role in European air traffic control developments through participation in a number of international fora. Britain has put forward a number of European initiatives, including the centralised management of traffic flows which is being progressively implemented over the period 1991–1995. Domestically, NATS has an investment programme currently running at around

£80 million a year, which includes the construction of a new air traffic control centre for England and Wales, due to be completed in 1996. Britain is a member of Eurocontrol, a European air traffic control body.

Aircraft and the Environment

The replacement of older aircraft by new quieter types has done much to reduce the problem of noise near airports, as have noise abatement measures such as noise-preferential routes, night restrictions and house insulation. Research is in hand on the effect of aircraft emissions on the upper atmosphere, and in the meantime consideration is being given internationally to tightening the emission standards for aircraft. The Government is considering taking reserve powers to require smaller airfields to agree noise reduction schemes.

Airports

Of the 144 licensed civil aerodromes in Britain, about one-fifth handle more than 100,000 passengers a year each. Twelve handle over 1 million passengers a year each (see Table 9). In 1990 Britain's civil airports handled a total of 104·1 million passengers (102·4 million terminal passengers and 1·7 million in transit), and 1·2 million tonnes of freight. Heathrow airport is the world's busiest airport for international travel and is Britain's most important airport for passengers and air freight, handling 43 million passengers (including transit passengers) and 695,300 tonnes of freight in 1990. Gatwick is one of the world's busiest international airports.

Ownership and Control

Seven airports—Heathrow, Gatwick, Stansted and Southampton in south-east England, and Glasgow, Edinburgh and Aberdeen in

Table 9: Passenger Traffic at Britain's Main Airports

Million passengers

	1985	1987	1988	1989	1990
London Heathrow	31·3	34·7	37·8	39·6	42·6
London Gatwick	14·9	19·3	20·8	21·1	21·0
Manchester	6·1	8·6	9·7	10·1	10·1
Glasgow	2·7	3·4	3·7	3·9	4·3
Birmingham	1·6	2·6	2·9	3·3	3·5
Luton	1·6	2·6	2·8	2·8	2·7
Edinburgh	1·6	1·8	2·1	2·4	2·5
Belfast Aldergrove	1·6	2·1	2·2	2·2	2·3
Aberdeen	1·7	1·5	1·6	1·7	1·9
Newcastle-upon-Tyne	1·0	1·3	1·4	1·5	1·6
East Midlands	0·9	1·3	1·3	1·5	1·3
London Stansted	0·5	0·7	1·0	1·3	1·2

Source: Civil Aviation Authority.
Note: Statistics relate to terminal passengers only and exclude those in transit.

Scotland—are owned and operated by BAA plc. Together they handle about 75 per cent of air passengers and 85 per cent of air cargo traffic in Britain. BAA plc was formerly publicly owned as the British Airports Authority, but was privatised in 1987.

Many of the other public airports are controlled by local authorities. A total of 15 major local authority airports now operate as Companies Act companies. The Government is encouraging the introduction of private capital into these new companies. For example, in May 1990 Liverpool Airport was sold to the private sector when British Aerospace acquired a controlling interest by the injection of new capital.

The CAA has responsibility for the economic regulation of major airport companies. It has powers to take action to remedy practices considered to be unreasonable or unfair, in particular any abuse of an airport's monopoly position. All airports used for public transport and training flights must be licensed by the CAA. Stringent requirements, such as the provision of adequate fire-fighting, medical and rescue services, must be satisfied before a licence is granted.

Development

The Government's policy is to promote a strong and competitive British airline industry by encouraging the provision of airport capacity where it is needed and by making effective use of existing capacity, including regional airports.

Major expansion is under way at Stansted. A new terminal was opened in March 1991, with an initial capacity of 8 million passengers a year. After further expansion it will cater for 15 million passengers a year. Under major expansion plans at Manchester, the first phase of a second terminal is under construction and is expected to open in 1993, increasing capacity by one-half to 18 million passengers a year. A second terminal at Birmingham was officially opened in 1991, increasing capacity to 6 million passengers a year. Facilities are also being improved at other regional airports.

Security

Strict security measures are in force. However, further steps have been taken to increase airport security in the wake of terrorist incidents worldwide. These include:

—the trial installation of machines at Heathrow and Gatwick to detect explosives in luggage;

—tighter checks on staff gaining access to restricted areas at airports;

—questioning of passengers about electrical equipment in their possession, and close examination of suspect devices; and

—the passage of the Aviation and Maritime Security Act 1990, which provides for greater powers to enforce security requirements and makes it an offence for travellers to give false information about baggage contents.

Channel Tunnel

Conception and Construction

Construction work is well under way on the Channel Tunnel, the largest civil engineering project in Europe to be financed by the private sector. Services in the twin single-track rail tunnel between Britain and France are expected to start in late 1993. The project, with a total financing requirement of over £8,000 million, is being undertaken by Eurotunnel, a British-French company.

The project was undertaken after a summit meeting between Britain and France in 1981, at which it was agreed that a joint study group be established to examine the technical and economic aspects of a fixed link. Following a favourable report, proposals were invited on the basis that no government funding or guarantee would be available. By late 1985, four schemes had been shortlisted. Two of these involved tunnels, one a bridge and the fourth a mixture of roadway and a tunnel between two artificial islands. The selection of the Eurotunnel plan was announced in January 1986. A treaty between the two countries was signed in February 1986 and ratified by both governments in July 1987. It regulates matters such as national jurisdiction, contains provisions to protect the public interest in matters such as safety and the environment, and sets out the private sector nature of the scheme. It also contains arrangements for arbitration in the event of a dispute over interpretation.

In March 1986 a concession agreement was signed between the two governments and the concessionaires, Eurotunnel. The agreement gives Eurotunnel the right to build the tunnel and operate it for a period of 55 years, after which its ownership will revert to the two governments. The agreement also stipulates that the governments will provide the necessary infrastructure and that Eurotunnel will be able to implement its own commercial policy on the service provided, including pricing. The project is being funded partly through bank borrowing and partly through equity funding in Britain and France.

The tunnel will consist of two single-track rail tunnels, each of 7·6 m (25 ft) in diameter, with a service tunnel of 4·8 m (16 ft) diameter between them. This service tunnel will provide access for maintenance and an evacuation route in an emergency. Construction is being carried out for Eurotunnel by Transmanche Link, a consortium of ten British and French construction companies. The first link-up under the Channel, that of the subsidiary service tunnel, took place in December 1990, and break-through of the two running tunnels was achieved in summer 1991.

Eurotunnel Services

Cars and lorries will be able to cross on specially-designed shuttle trains, which will provide a regular no-booking, drive-on, drive-off service at frequent intervals round the clock. Eurotunnel has ordered 17 shuttle trains, nine for passenger vehicles and eight for freight vehicles.

Vehicles will be loaded at the two terminals being constructed at either end of the tunnel, one near Folkestone and the other near Calais. Trains will be formed of one or two 'rakes' of enclosed carrier wagons. A rake of double-decked wagons will carry an average of 108 cars, while a rake of single-decked wagons will carry about 54 cars or 12 coaches. Track loops at each terminal will allow the shuttle trains to enter and leave the stations without reversing. Drivers will normally stay with their cars for the crossing, which will take about 35 minutes; the overall transit time in normal traffic conditions through the system from arriving at the toll booths at one terminal and driving off at the other is expected to be between 50 and 80 minutes on most days of the year. There will be attendants on board the wagons to ensure that safety regulations are complied with and to assist passengers in the event of an emergency.

Rail Services

In order to cope with the extra traffic that will be generated by the opening of the Channel Tunnel, BR plans to invest some £1,400 million in new passenger and freight rolling stock and infrastructure. Of this, over £800 million has already been approved by the Secretary of State for Transport.

Improvements that are being made to existing facilities include:

—a new passenger terminal at London Waterloo;

—a new international station at Ashford in Kent;

—electrification of the route from Redhill to Tonbridge, which will carry freight to the tunnel; and

—electrification of the West London Line, which will provide access to the North.

Some 30 high-speed through passenger services are planned to run each day between London Waterloo and Paris, and London and Brussels. These trains will be considerably longer than those for domestic services; their 18 coaches will stretch for almost 400 metres (430 yards). It will take about 3 hours to travel from London to Paris and, once a Belgian high-speed line is completed in the mid-1990s, about 2 hours 40 minutes to travel to Brussels. Through day-passenger services from the Midlands, northern England and Scotland to the continent are planned; these will require a specially adapted version of the international rolling stock, but these will not be ready before 1994.

New regional depots are planned to handle freight traffic to the continent. BR anticipates that a high proportion of freight traffic through the tunnel will be 'intermodal'. Such traffic uses 'swap bodies', wagon bodies that can either be mounted on railway wheels or hauled directly by lorries. New wagon technology will enable BR to accept standard European swap bodies and containers while still operating within the standard British loading gauge. New designs of intermodal wagon with a lower floor structure will enable demountable units up to 2·67 m (8 ft 9 ins) to be carried within the present British loading gauge. New wagon designs, including the use of lower loading decks, are being explored. The tunnel will also allow BR to offer improved parcel services.

To meet the forecast growth in demand for through rail services, additional capacity will be required between the Channel Tunnel and London by about the year 2005. It is proposed to construct a fast rail link and a second London passenger terminal to meet this need. Following a review of possible routes, the Government announced in October 1991 that it had selected King's Cross as the site for the second terminal. Its preferred route for the line to King's Cross approaches London from the east, crossing the River Thames in a tunnel from Kent to Essex and travelling via Stratford in east London. This should help ensure that the economic benefits of the Channel Tunnel do not affect just the South East, but are spread to other regions. The Government intends the fast link project to be taken forward by the private sector.

Telecommunications

The telecommunications industry is one of the most rapidly growing sectors of the British economy. Major changes occurred in the
1980s with the progressive introduction of competition into the
markets for telecommunications equipment and services. In 1984
British Telecommunications (BT) was privatised, and has faced
competition in the provision of services over fixed links from
Mercury Communications. Competitive mobile, satellite and data
services have been licensed. The Telecommunications Act 1984
established a regulatory regime, the main feature of which is the
establishment of an independent industry regulator, the Director
General of Telecommunications.

Duopoly Review

In 1991 a major review of government telecommunications policy
resulted in the publication of a White Paper, *Competition and
Choice: Telecommunications Policy for the 1990s*. This stated that the
Government would consider sympathetically applications from
companies wishing to run fixed telecommunications networks,
ending the so-called 'duopoly policy', under which only BT and
Mercury were permitted to run such systems. By December 1991
the Government had received 17 applications of this kind. Other
important points of the review were:

—greater freedom for existing mobile telecommunications opera-
    tors and the ability of cable television operators to provide ser-
    vices in their own right;

—more effective and streamlined procedures for the interconnection of systems, giving OFTEL (see below) the power to set
interconnection terms where agreement could not be reached
between the parties;

—the introduction of 'equal access', by which customers can exer-
cise choice over the trunk operator that carries their calls;

—the introduction of new class licences for satellite systems and to
enable companies to build and operate their own telecommunications systems; and

—the establishment of a new national numbering scheme, and the
modification of operators' licences to allow for the introduction
of number portability.

The Government concluded that it would be unlikely to license any
new facilities-based international operators in the short term.
However, the resale of capacity on international leased circuits has
already been liberalised where this involves the conveyance of messages over a circuit connected to the public network at one end
only. In addition, the Government is discussing with other countries the possibility of liberalising international simple resale—that
is, where messages are conveyed over an international leased circuit
connected to the public network at both ends.

Office of Telecommunications

The Office of Telecommunications (OFTEL), a non-ministerial
government department, is the independent regulatory body for
the telecommunications industry. It is headed by the Director
General of Telecommunications, among whose functions are to:

—ensure that licensees comply with the conditions of their licences;

—initiate the amendment of licence conditions by agreement or by a reference to the Monopolies and Mergers Commission;

—to promote effective competition in the telecommunications industry;

—to provide advice to the Secretary of State for Trade and Industry on telecommunications matters; and

—to investigate complaints.

The Director General also has a duty to promote the interests of consumers in respect of prices, quality and variety in telecommunications services.

BT

The telephone service in Britain was set up in the nineteenth century, partly by the Post Office but also by private companies. In 1889 the main private companies combined to form the National Telephone Company, which became part of the Post Office at the end of 1911. From 1912, therefore, the Post Office had, with few exceptions, a statutory monopoly on Britain's telecommunications. However, under the British Telecommunications Act 1981, the telecommunications business was split off as British Telecommunications. In 1984 BT was reconstituted as a public limited company and a majority of the ordinary voting shares were sold to private investors. In May 1991 it had about 1·1 million registered shareholders. Some 90 per cent of its 230,000 employees own shares and nearly 44 per cent are members of the Employee Share Save Scheme. The Government sold some of its remaining

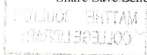

shares by means of a public offer in November 1991; it retains about 22 per cent of the total.

BT runs one of the world's largest public telecommunications networks, including:

—19·6 million residential lines;

—6 million business lines;

—78,200 telex connections;

—98,200 public payphones; and

—a wide range of specialised voice, data, text and visual services.

The inland telephone and telex networks are fully automatic. International direct dialling is available from Britain to 200 countries, representing 99 per cent of the world's telephones. Automatic telex service is available to more than 200 countries.

Network Modernisation

BT is investing some £11 million per working day in the modernisation and expansion of its network to meet the increasing demand for basic telephone services and for more specialised services. The company has more than 1·4 million km (870,000 miles) of optical fibre laid in its network in Britain, a higher proportion than any other world operator. There are more than 3,650 digital exchanges serving some 73 per cent of telephone lines. The combination of digital exchange switching and digital transmission techniques, using optical fibre cable and microwave radio links, is substantially improving the quality of telephone services for residential and business customers, as well as making possible a wider range of services through the company's main network.

General Services

BT's services include:

—a free facility for emergency calls to the police, fire, ambulance, coastguard, lifeboat and air-sea rescue services;

—directory enquiries;

—various chargeable operator-connected services, such as reverse-charge calls and alarm calls;

—an operator-handled Freefone service and automatic 'LinkLine' facilities that enable callers to contact organisations anywhere in Britain, either free or at local call rates;

—a number of Callstream services, which allow callers to obtain information by paying a premium call rate; and

—network services such as three-way calling, call waiting and call diversion, which are available to customers on digital exchanges.

Other premium-rate services are offered by independent service providers using the BT network. In 1988 the company opened a £70 million optical fibre flexible access system, for intensive voice and data traffic, to serve the financial organisations of the City of London.

Under a public payphone service modernisation programme, a total of £165 million is being spent on modernisation and additional provision on sites convenient for travellers, such as railway stations and motorway service areas. A number of cashless call developments are being carried out, including the Phonecard service, using prepaid encoded cards; Phonecard payphones account for 19,000 of the total of 98,200 payphones. There are about 280,000 private rented payphones on premises to which the public has access and these are also being upgraded with modern push-button equipment.

Prestel, BT's videotex service, and Telecom Gold (an electronic mail and information service) form part of the company's data services division, BT Tymnet Europe. Prestel was the first service of its kind to enable a wide variety of electronically-stored information to be called up via the telephone on a computer, a terminal or an adapted television. Some 100,000 terminals are attached to Prestel, primarily in businesses. Through its 'gateway' links with other databases, a wide range of other services, such as home shopping and banking services, holiday booking and reservation facilities, and insurance and financial markets information, is available.

International Services

BT has much experience as an international network and service provider. It is the second largest shareholder in the International Telecommunications Satellite Organisation (of which 120 countries are members) and in the European Telecommunications Satellite Organisation. It is also a leading shareholder in the International Maritime Satellite Organisation, with interests in a number of other consortia.

A substantial proportion of the intercontinental telephone traffic to or from Britain is carried by satellite. BT operates satellite earth stations in the London Docklands and at Goonhilly Downs (Cornwall), Madley (near Hereford) and Aberdeen. Its range of digital transmission services includes a number available overseas, including 'Satstream' private circuit digital links covering North America and Western Europe using small-dish aerials, and an 'International Kilostream' private circuit service available to the

United States, Australia and most major business centres in Asia and the rest of Europe. Extensive direct-dial maritime satellite services are available for vessels worldwide. In-flight operator-controlled telephone call facilities are available via Portishead radio station near Bristol. Digital transmission techniques have been introduced for services to the United States, Japan, Hong Kong and Australia via the Madley and Goonhilly stations. The London-Tokyo link, which was set up in 1986, includes the first all-digital telephone link between two continents.

Recent improvements in submarine cable design (including the use of optical fibre technology) have helped to increase capacity and reduce pressure on satellite systems. A second high-capacity transatlantic optical fibre cable (TAT 9), which is able to carry about 75,000 telephone calls simultaneously, came into operation in March 1992 to supplement an earlier link.

BT's overseas consultancy service, Telconsult, has so far completed 270 projects in more than 60 countries.

Mercury Communications

Mercury Communications Ltd, a wholly-owned subsidiary of Cable & Wireless plc, is licensed as a public telecommunications operator in Britain. Mercury has constructed its own long-distance all-digital network comprising over 3,000 km (1,850 miles) of optical fibre cables and 2,700 km (1,680 miles) of digital microwave links. The network runs from the north of Scotland to the south coast, serving some 88 towns and cities across Britain. Coverage is enhanced through Mercury's own city cable networks as well as partnerships with local cable television operators. Service is also provided over microwave connections.

Mercury offers a full range of long-distance and international telecommunications services for both business and residential customers. In addition to voice and data transmission, the company supplies advanced messaging systems, mobile telecommunications and a range of equipment for customers' premises. Major customers can have a direct digital link between their premises and the Mercury network. A number of routeing devices have also been developed to enable customers to use Mercury indirectly via their existing exchange lines. Residential customers can buy a Mercury-compatible phone with push-button access to the service.

International services are provided by satellite communications centres in the London Docklands and in Oxfordshire, as well as by submarine cable links to the continent of Europe and the United States.

Mobile Communications

The Government has strongly encouraged the expansion of mobile telecommunications services. It has licensed Vodafone Ltd and Telecom Securicor Cellular Radio Ltd to run competing national cellular radio systems. Considerable investment has been made in establishing their networks to provide increased capacity for the growing number of cellular radio telephone users (over 1·2 million by the end of 1991). The two companies will also run the new pan-European mobile system in Britain.

Britain will be the first country to offer personal communications network (PCN) services, which are intended to allow the same telephone to be used at home, at work and as a portable wherever there is network capacity. In 1991 the Government issued licences to three operators—Mercury Personal Communications Ltd,

Microtel Communications Ltd and Unitel Ltd to run PCNs in the frequency range around 1·8 gigahertz.

Two operators, GEC National One and Band 3 Radio Ltd, have been licensed to offer a nationwide trunked radio service, while a number of licences have been awarded for London and regional services. Licences have also been granted to a number of companies to run nationwide paging and mobile data networks.

Cable Television

The Government has licensed 119 companies that were awarded local cable television franchises to run broadband cable telecommunications systems. The 45 systems in operation provide television programmes, but some are already offering interactive services, including local voice telephony. The Government concluded in the duopoly review that cable operators should be able to offer voice telephony in their own right; previously this could only be provided in conjunction with BT or Mercury.

Cable & Wireless

Cable & Wireless plc provides a wide range of telecommunications in some 50 countries worldwide. Its main business is the provision and operation of public telecommunications services in over 30 countries and territories, including the United States, Japan and Hong Kong, under franchises and licences granted by the governments concerned. It also provides and manages telecommunications services and facilities for public and private sector customers, and undertakes consultancy work. It operates a fleet of 11 ships and three submersible vehicle systems for laying and maintaining submarine telecommunications cables. In recent years the company has been constructing and bringing into service a broadband digital network linking major world economic and financial centres in Europe, north America and the Pacific Rim. The first leg of this 'Global Digital Highway', the private transatlantic optical fibre cable linking Britain, the Irish Republic, the United States and Bermuda, entered service in 1989. The North Pacific Cable, the first direct cable between the United States and Japan, entered service in 1991, connecting to other optical fibre cables in the Pacific Rim region. Cable & Wireless is pursuing a strategy of providing premium services for business customers, expanding basic telecommunications services and building up mobile communications businesses around the world.

Postal Services

Development of Postal Services

Britain's Post Office pioneered postal services and was the first to issue adhesive postage stamps as proof of advance payment for mail. The public mail service goes back to 1635, when King Charles I decreed that his subjects might use his Royal Mail upon payment. As a result of the opening up of the service, more postal routes were set up. From the late eighteenth century, the post was carried on mail coaches, each one accompanied by an armed guard for protection against highwaymen. Carrying the mail was a royal monopoly, although important towns in Britain were allowed to set up local post networks.

The Post Office was transformed in the 1840s by two developments—the spread of railways, which replaced mail coaches, and the invention of the penny post by Rowland Hill (1795–1879). Previously the cost of postage had been paid by the recipient, not the sender, and prices varied by distance. Prices could thus be very high. Rowland Hill suggested that there should instead be a flat rate of one old penny for all inland letters up to half an ounce in weight, paid in advance. As proof of payment, he suggested the use of stamps that could be stuck onto letters and franked by the postmaster to prevent re-use. The world's first stamp, the 'Penny Black', went on sale in May 1840, and other countries were swift to copy the innovation. With the introduction in the 1850s of pillar boxes for people to post their letters more conveniently than at a post office—a suggestion of Anthony Trollope (1815–82), the famous novelist, who was working for the Post Office at the time—the basic features of the modern postal system were in use.

The Post Office Today

Today, the Royal Mail provides deliveries to 25 million addresses and handles over 60 million letters and parcels each working day, which comes to over 15,000 million items a year. Some 166 million parcels were handled in 1990–91. Mail is collected from over 100,000 posting boxes, as well as from post offices and large postal users. Capital investment of £1,600 million over a five-year period is planned. The Post Office Group is divided into three main businesses: Royal Mail, Parcelforce and Post Office Counters.

Inland Mail

Good progress has been made in modernising the letters business. Mail sorting was traditionally done by hand at some 600 offices of varying size and capacity. During the past 20 years, however, much of the process has been mechanised and concentrated into larger offices. Some 80 such mechanised letter offices are now in operation. The machines at mechanised sorting offices are capable of segregating letters from parcels, of getting letters all facing the same way and automatically franking the mail.

At the heart of mechanised sorting operations, however, is the postcode system. This was introduced between 1966 and 1974, following extensive trials. It is the most sophisticated in the world, allowing mechanised sorting down to part of a street on a postman's round and, in some cases, to an individual address. The code consists of two groups of letters and figures, the first of which enables the letter to be directed to the office at its destination. The second group enables the machines there to sort the letter for delivery. Since the early 1980s optical character recognition machines have been introduced, which are able to read typed and printed post-codes and add codes, in the form of phosphor dots, which the sorting machines can read. About three-quarters of mail now carries the postcode.

International Mail

Britain has good international postal services, with prices among the cheapest and more direct flights to the rest of the world than any other country. Royal Mail International dispatches 600 million items a year, including more than 400 million by air. It has its own terminal building at Heathrow, opened in 1989, which handles some four-fifths of outward airmail. It uses 1,400 flights every week to send mail direct to over 300 destinations worldwide.

Parcelforce

The Post Office has handled parcels since the establishment of the parcels post in 1883. The present parcels operation, Parcelforce, has a programme of modernisation, including the establishment of 150 local collection and delivery depots throughout Britain. It is becoming more independent from the letters service—hence the move to set up its own specialist depots rather than sharing with the letters offices. However, in rural areas it will continue to sub-contract delivery to the letters service. It has also re-organised its structure, previously based on 11 geographical divisions, into six new management areas, each with fewer staff than one of the old districts.

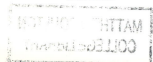

Post Office Counters

There are 20,600 post offices, of which some 1,200 are operated directly by the Post Office. The remainder are operated on an agency basis by sub-postmasters. The counters business handles a wide range of transactions; it acts as an agent for the letters and parcels businesses, government departments, local authorities and Girobank, which was transferred to the private sector in July 1990.

Considerable investment is being made in updating and improving the service in post offices. The aim is to cut queueing times so that no-one has to wait more than five minutes. Increased computerisation is helping counter clerks to handle transactions more quickly. There are now more than 350 stamp vending machines in main offices, which further helps to reduce queues. Experiments have also been started in reducing the number of transactions carried out behind screens by moving towards a more open-plan office.

Post Office Specialist Services

The Post Office provides a range of specialist services. 'Datapost', a door-to-door delivery service, has overnight links throughout Britain and provides an international service to over 160 countries. 'Datapost Sameday' provides a rapid delivery within or between more than 100 cities and towns in Britain and between London and Amsterdam, Paris and Dublin. The Philatelic Bureau in Edinburgh handles about one-third of the Post Office's philatelic business, much of it involving sales to overseas collectors or dealers. The British Postal Consultancy Service offers advice and assistance on all aspects of postal business to overseas postal

administrations, and some 50 countries have used its services since 1965.

Introduction of Competition

The Post Office still has a monopoly on delivering letters. However, the Secretary of State for Trade and Industry has the power to suspend this monopoly in certain areas or for certain categories of mail, and to license others to provide competing services. Under these powers, the Government has:

—suspended the monopoly on letters subject to a minimum fee of £1;

—issued general licences enabling mail to be transferred between document exchanges; and

—allowed charitable organisations to carry Christmas and New Year cards.

As part of the Citizen's Charter published in July 1991, the Government proposed that the level below which the Post Office has a monopoly on letter delivery should be reduced from the current £1 fee to a figure much nearer the cost of a first-class letter (presently 24 pence). The Government's policy is that there should continue to be a universal letter service with a uniform and affordable tariff structure. However, it is proposed to introduce competition by three principal routes:

—the reduction of the present £1 letter monopoly to a level much closer to the price of a first-class stamp, as proposed in the Citizen's Charter;

—an extended discount system, so that the Post Office would offer further discounts to those who do the additional work of trunking their mail as far as the final delivery office; and

—the licensing of 'niche' services under the monopoly limit.

Under these proposals, service standards would be decided not by the Post Office as at present, but by the Secretary of State. He would be advised on this by a new regulator, who would also advise on ways of preventing the Post Office from cross-subsidising its services in ways which may be unfair to its competitors or to specific groups of customers.

Private Courier and Express Service Operators

Private sector couriers and express operators are able to handle door-to-door deliveries, subject to the £1 minimum fee presently needed to avoid the Post Office monopoly. As a result of the demand for rapid delivery of urgent items, the courier/express service industry has grown rapidly, by about 20 per cent a year. The revenue created by the carriage of these items is estimated at over £1,500 million a year. Britain is one of the main providers of monitored express deliveries in Europe, with London an important centre for air courier/express traffic.

Addresses

Department of the Environment, 2 Marsham Street, London SW1P 3EB.

Department of Trade and Industry, Ashdown House, 123 Victoria Street, London SW1E 6RB.

Department of Transport, 2 Marsham Street, London SW1P 3EB.

Northern Ireland Office, Stormont Castle, Belfast BT4 3ST.

Scottish Office, St Andrew's House, Edinburgh EH1 3DE.

Welsh Office, Cathays Park, Cardiff CF1 1NQ.

Associated British Ports Holdings plc, 150 Holborn, London EC1N 2LR.

BAA plc, 130 Wilton Road, London SW1V 1LQ.

British Airways plc, Heathrow Airport, Hounslow TW6 2JA.

British Rail, Euston House, 24 Eversholt Street, London NW1 1DZ.

British Telecommunications plc, 81 Newgate Street, London EC1A 7AT.

British Waterways Board, Greycaine Road, Watford WD2 4JP.

Cable & Wireless, New Mercury House, 26 Red Lion Square, London WC1R 4UQ.

Civil Aviation Authority, CAA House, 45-59 Kingsway, London WC2B 6TE.

London Transport, 55 Broadway, London SW1H 0BD.

Mercury Communications Ltd, New Mercury House, 26 Red Lion Square, London WC1R 4OQ.

Oftel, Export House, 50 Ludgate Hill, London EC4M 7JJ.

Post Office, 30 St James's Square, London SW1Y 4PY.

Further Reading

£

Bus and Coach Statistics Great Britain 1990–91.
Department of Transport.
ISBN 0 11 551081 8.   HMSO   11·20

Competition and Choice: Telecommunications Policy for the 1990s.
Department of Trade and Industry.
Cm 1461. ISBN 0 10 114612 4.   HMSO   8·65

The Government's Expenditure Plans 1991–92 to 1993–94:
Department of Trade and Industry.
Cm 1904. ISBN 0 10 119042 5.   HMSO   7·70

Department of Transport.
Cm 1907. ISBN 0 10 119072 7.   HMSO   14·60

Merchant Fleet Statistics 1991.
Department of Transport.
ISBN 0 11 551106 7.   HMSO   19·60

Road Traffic Act 1991.
Department of Transport circular 1991/4.
ISBN 0 11 551093 1.   HMSO   2·85

		£
Telephone Service in 1991.	Oftel	Free

*The Transport of Goods by Road in Great
Britain 1990: Annual Report of the Continuing
Survey of Road Goods Transport.*
Department of Transport.
ISBN 0 11 551089 3.   HMSO   12·00

Transport Statistics Great Britain 1991.
Department of Transport.
ISBN 0 11 551078 8.   HMSO   24·00

Written by Reference Services,
Central Office of Information.

Printed in the United Kingdom for HMSO.
Dd 0294182, 7/92, C30, 51-2423, 5673.